CODE RED
OCTOBER 8, 1871
The Great Chicago Fire

by Janet McHugh

Consultant: Sarah S. Marcus
Historian, Chicago History Museum

BEARPORT
PUBLISHING

New York, New York

Credits

Cover and Title Page, © The Granger Collection, New York; 3, © Stock Montage/Getty Images; 4, © Chicago Historical Society; 6, © Smithsonian Institution; 7, © Stock Montage/Getty Images; 9, © Stock Montage/Getty Images; 10T, © Chicago Public Library; 10B, © Chicago Public Library; 11, © Chicago Historical Society, ICHi-50234; 12, © Chicago Historical Society, i02897aa; 13T, © Chicago Historical Society, i02990; 13B, © Chicago Historical Society, i12456; 14, © Chicago Public Library; 15, © Chicago Public Library; 16, © Chicago Historical Society, i02881; 17, © Chicago Historical Society, i02889; 18, © North Wind Picture Archives; 19, © Chicago Historical Society, i14894aa; 20, © Chicago Public Library; 21, © Chicago Historical Society, i02254; 22-23, © Bettmann/Corbis; 24, © Brown Brothers; 25, © Stock Montage; 26, © Bettmann/Corbis; 27, © Stock Montage; 28T, © Mansell/Time & Life Pictures/Getty Images; 28B, © Chicago Historical Society, i31917; 29T, © Chicago Historical Society, i34703aa; 29B, © Chicago Historical Society, i12924; 29 Background, © Brown Brothers; 30-31, © Brown Brothers.

Publisher: Kenn Goin
Editorial Director: Adam Siegel
Creative Director: Spencer Brinker
Photo Researcher: Marty Levick
Design: Dawn Beard Creative

Library of Congress Cataloging-in-Publication Data

McHugh, Janet.
  The great Chicago fire / by Janet McHugh.
    p. cm. — (Code red)
  Includes bibliographical references and index.
  ISBN-13: 978-1-59716-360-6 (library binding)
  ISBN-10: 1-59716-360-0 (library binding)
  1. Great Fire, Chicago, Ill., 1871—Juvenile literature. 2. Fires—Illinois—Chicago—History—
19th century—Juvenile literature. 3. Chicago (Ill.)—History—To 1875—Juvenile literature.
I. Title.

  F548.42.M217 2007
  977.3'1103—dc22

                            2006026706

For more information, write to Bearport Publishing Company, Inc., 101 Fifth Avenue, Suite 6R, New York, New York 10003. Printed in the United States of America.

10 9 8 7 6 5 4 3 2 1

Contents

A Night of Terror

It was Monday, October 9, 1871, in Chicago, Illinois. At 2:00 in the morning, Mary Fales woke suddenly. She heard carts and wagons rolling past her house. From the window, she saw a strange glow lighting up the night sky.

The evening before, Mary heard that a fire had started in another part of the city. She and her husband, David, went to bed thinking they would be safe. Now, however, wind was spreading the flames. Soon the fire would reach their neighborhood!

Terrified, Mary and David packed their belongings in a horse-drawn **buggy**. Climbing aboard, they joined the crowds trying to escape.

Bridges became choked with people, animals, and carts as everyone fled for safety.

Each year, Fire Prevention Week takes place across the United States during the week of October 9, in memory of the Great Chicago Fire.

66 I had to use all my powers to keep going on. I was glad to go fast, for the fire behind us raged and the whole earth . . . was . . . yellowish red. 99

–Mary Fales, in a letter she wrote to her mother

Where Is the Fire Department?

The Great Chicago Fire started around 9:00 on Sunday evening, October 8. It began in or near a barn on Chicago's southwest side.

A fire watchman tried to identify the fire's location. Unfortunately, he made a mistake. He sent firefighters to the wrong place. By the time they finally arrived at the barn, the flames had spread to many buildings.

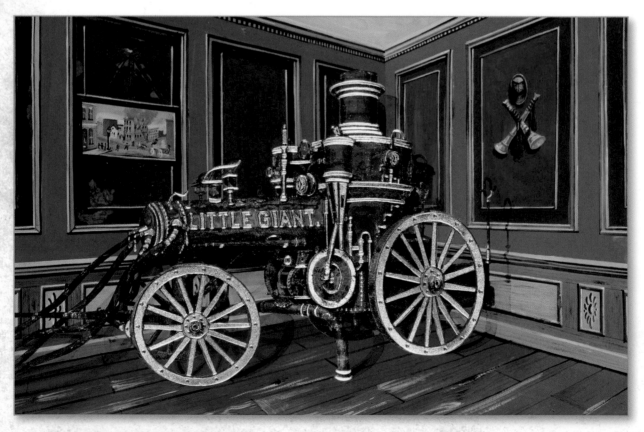

Pulled by its four horses, the *Little Giant* was one of the first fire engines to reach the fire. It soon lost its battle trying to put out the flames.

The Chicago Fire Department had only 185 firefighters to protect the city. Many of the firefighters were exhausted. Half of them had just spent Saturday night through Sunday afternoon battling another big fire. Despite their efforts, they could not stop the new flames from spreading.

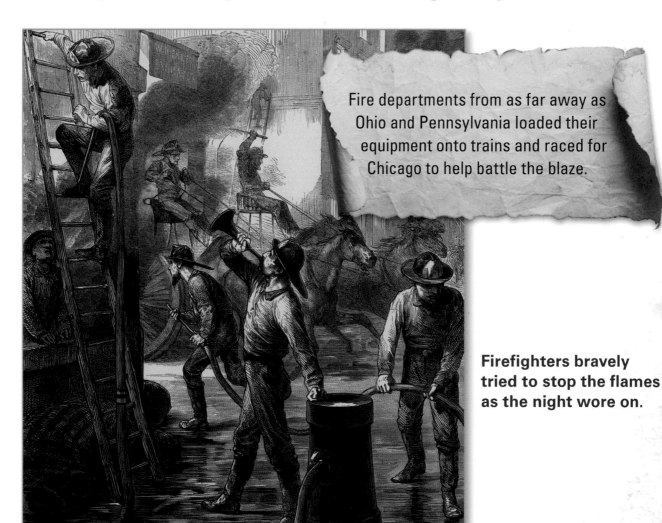

Fire departments from as far away as Ohio and Pennsylvania loaded their equipment onto trains and raced for Chicago to help battle the blaze.

Firefighters bravely tried to stop the flames as the night wore on.

"CHICAGO IS IN FLAMES. SEND YOUR WHOLE DEPARTMENT TO HELP US."

—Roswell B. Mason, mayor of Chicago, in a telegram sent to the mayor of Milwaukee, Wisconsin

"Fire Devils"

At first, the fire was only burning west of the Chicago River. Everyone hoped the fire would stop at the water's edge.

Unfortunately, hot air rose from the flames and mixed with the cool air above it, creating **convection whirls**. Witnesses called them "fire devils." A fire devil could pick up a burning piece of wood and send it flying. New fires started where the flaming objects landed.

The city of Chicago runs along several miles of Lake Michigan's sandy shore. The Chicago River flows through the city.

No photographs exist of the Chicago fire. Perhaps the intense heat made taking photos impossible. Or perhaps the flames burned up all the cameras and film that were used that night.

At about 11:30 P.M. on Sunday, fire devils sent burning **debris** flying over the river! Flames began to spread through the city. The small fire department and limited equipment were powerless to stop them.

Flames and smoke leaped out of Crosby's Opera House and spread to nearby buildings.

66 The fire was coming down thicker than any snowstorm you ever saw.... 99

–William B. Bateham, as he watched a furniture factory burning on his property

The Warning Bell

Bong, bong, bong. The bell at the top of the courthouse warned people of the fire. Here, high above the ground, watchmen anxiously tracked the flames heading toward them. In offices below, city officials directed firefighting efforts. In the basement, prisoners in the city jail begged to be set free.

The courthouse also served as Chicago's city hall and its jail.

Here is the courthouse after the fire. The watchtower and center section were completely destroyed.

At about 1:30 Monday morning, sparks set the courthouse tower on fire. As the bell kept tolling, the watchmen and city officials fled. First, though, they released the prisoners into the street.

Soon fire swept through the building. The bell crashed to the ground. Its deafening sound could be heard all over Chicago.

The courthouse bell was later melted down and molded into tiny bells. The makers sold these "charm bells" as fire **souvenirs**.

A charm bell made from the courthouse bell

Looting in the Streets

The flames continued to spread, destroying businesses and homes. Some people were taking advantage of the confusion caused by the fire. A wave of **looting** broke out! Thieves smashed into locked stores and deserted homes. They grabbed all the **goods** they could carry. Nothing was safe.

Looters stole whiskey from Chicago's many saloons.

Finally, Mayor Roswell B. Mason placed the city under **martial law**. He called in the army to stop the looters. Yet the army wasn't the only thing stopping the thieves. As the fire grew worse, many people had to drop their stolen goods and run from the deadly flames. Their loot was left to burn in the street.

After the fire, U.S. soldiers patrolled Chicago's streets to protect them from looters.

Civil War hero General Philip H. Sheridan was put in charge of martial law in Chicago.

No More Water!

A fierce wind from the south drove the fire northward. Ahead lay the city's **waterworks**. From this castle-like stone building, large pumps drew water from Lake Michigan. The waterworks pumped the water to the top of the 154-foot (47-m) water tower. From there, the water flowed out through pipes to places around the city. Firefighters used water pumped from the building to battle the flames.

The waterworks (right) and water tower (center) before the fire

At about 3:20 Monday morning, the wind sent a flaming piece of **timber** sailing onto the roof of the waterworks. Within minutes, the wooden part of the roof was **ablaze**. It soon collapsed, cutting off the flow of water. Fire hoses went limp and dry. The last hope to stop the mighty blaze had dried up, too.

"You couldn't see anything over you but fire.... No clouds, no stars, nothing else but fire.**"**

–Thomas Byrne, firefighter battling the flames

The water tower and waterworks are the only public buildings in downtown Chicago that survived the fire. Today, they stand as historic landmarks on Chicago's Michigan Avenue.

Where to Flee?

"Run for your lives!" a man on horseback racing through the streets called out. People wanted to obey the call. Where, though, would they be safe?

Thousands headed for the shore of Lake Michigan. Many buried themselves in sand there. They left small air holes to breathe through. Other people **waded** out chest-deep into the lake.

Thousands fled from the flames through a cemetery. They were headed to Lincoln Park, a large open area.

Mary and David Fales thought they had found safety on the north side of the city. Soon, though, flames threatened them there. Once again, they had to **flee**. They raced toward the open **prairie** west of the city. There they sadly joined thousands of other homeless **refugees**.

Tired and homeless, people rested among the ruins of the city.

Hundreds of horses and dogs gathered on the shore of Lake Michigan to keep safe from the flames.

At Last, the Rain!

By late Monday night, the fire had been raging for more than 25 hours. Yet there was still one thing that might be able to stop it—rain.

Safe at last from the flames, crowded refugees camped out on Lake Michigan's shore.

At about 11:00 that night, a cold drizzle began to fall. It grew heavier as the night went on. By Tuesday morning, rain finally drowned the last glowing **embers** in the city. Though now wet and chilled, the people of Chicago were relieved and thankful. The fire was over.

> 66 I never felt so grateful in my life as to hear the rain pour down. 99
>
> —Mary Fales, Great Chicago Fire survivor

The Great Chicago Fire of 1871 burned its way across an area more than four miles (6.4 km) long and almost one mile (1.6 km) wide.

A Fire Waiting to Happen

How could such a terrible fire happen? Rapid city growth and dry weather were partly to blame.

Chicago had grown quickly since its founding in 1833. The population had swelled from a few hundred people to 334,000 the year of the fire. Thousands of wooden buildings had been built to house all the people.

Chicago had been built on swampy land, so the ground was often muddy. The city built miles of wooden streets and sidewalks. Many of these went up in flames during the fire.

In the three months before the fire, Chicago got much less rain than usual. All that wood grew very dry. It became extremely **flammable**.

On the evening of October 8, 1871, a fire started in or near a barn that belonged to Kate and Patrick O'Leary. Somehow, the hay they used to feed their cows caught fire. With so many dry, wooden buildings nearby, the flames quickly spread. Soon the city of Chicago was ablaze.

The O'Leary barn was destroyed in the fire. Yet the family's home, shown here, survived.

For more than 100 years after the fire, a **legend** grew that a cow angrily kicked over a lantern as Mrs. O'Leary tried to milk her. Mrs. O'Leary, however, stubbornly denied the charge that her cow had started the fire.

A City in Ruins

As dawn broke on Tuesday morning, the **weary** people of Chicago looked out over their city. A sad new song captured what they saw: *"Ruins! Ruins! Far and wide from the river and lake to the prairie side."*

In the rush to escape the fire, many families had become separated. Now anxious husbands searched for their missing wives. Worried mothers searched for their missing children.

Fearing the worst, many people approached a **morgue** set up for the fire's victims. Every minute, ten people were allowed through its doors. They dreaded finding their loved ones lying there among the dead.

The fire killed about 300 people, destroyed more than 17,500 buildings, and left around 100,000 people homeless.

Picking Up the Pieces

Chicago's citizens immediately set out to rebuild their lives. First, many had to replace their lost homes. In just one week, they put up about 6,000 **temporary** shacks. A homemade sign on one of the shacks said: "ALL GONE BUT WIFE, CHILDREN AND ENERGY." **Soup kitchens** sprang up to offer simple meals to the hungry.

After the fire, small shacks were built as temporary homes.

66 When . . . I knew I had my husband and my children safe, I felt so rich— I have never in my life felt so rich! 99

—Mrs. Charles Forsberg, a fire survivor

Help poured in from the rest of the country. New York City collected clothing from its citizens to send to Chicago. Milwaukee and St. Louis sent trainloads of relief supplies. People from Cincinnati set up a soup kitchen that fed 3,500 people a day.

Supplies from New York were sent to survivors of the fire.

In 1997, the Chicago City Council decided to investigate how the fire began. Based on all the facts they looked at, the council said Kate O'Leary and her cow were innocent.

"Chicago Shall Rise Again!"

The great fire destroyed many of Chicago's businesses. The owners, however, did not give up. Within six months, Marshall Field rebuilt his famous department store. Nearby, Potter Palmer replaced his burned-out Palmer House with an even more elegant hotel. The **housing boom** drew construction workers from all over the country.

The World's Columbian Exposition covered more than 600 acres (243 hectares) of Chicago's waterfront. Its white buildings earned it the nickname the White City.

Just over twenty years later, the people of Chicago wanted to show off their new city. In 1893, the city hosted the World's Columbian Exposition. It was a huge fair to honor the 400th anniversary of Christopher Columbus's coming to the Americas. About 27 million visitors came to celebrate the Exposition—and Chicago's amazing rebirth.

The 1893 Exposition introduced the world to a brand-new invention—the Ferris wheel. Today, another Ferris wheel like this one still stands along Chicago's lakefront.

66 All is not lost. Chicago still exists. She was not a mere collection of stones, and bricks, and lumber. . . . *Chicago Shall Rise Again.* 99

–Joseph Medill, publisher of the *Chicago Tribune*, three days after the fire

27

Many people played an important role in the events connected to the Great Chicago Fire. Here are four of them.

Thomas Hughes **was a famous British writer.**

- Supported the English Book Donation, a plan to send books to Chicago from England after the fire
- Helped collect about 7,000 books from English writers, publishers, and booksellers
- Helped create the Free Public Library of Chicago, the first public library in the city's history

Roswell B. Mason **was the mayor of Chicago from 1869 to 1871.**

- Worked as an engineer to build railroads before he was elected mayor
- Praised by some for the common sense and brave character he showed during the disaster
- Spent his final months in office trying to help the fire refugees

Kate O'Leary was blamed by some people for accidentally starting the fire.

- Before the fire, kept five cows in her barn and sold their milk in the neighborhood
- Denied that she and one of her cows were guilty of starting the fire
- Refused to let a photograph of her be taken because she did not want it to be shown when she was blamed for the fire

Fire Marshal Robert A. Williams was head of the Chicago Fire Department.

- Before the fire, tried to get Chicago's city government to provide more firefighters and equipment
- Interviewed by the *Chicago Tribune* as part of an investigation of the fire
- Criticized for not being able to control the fire

Glossary

ablaze (uh-BLAZE) on fire

buggy (BUHG-ee) a small carriage pulled by a horse

convection whirls (kuhn-VEK-shuhn WURLZ) spinning movements of air caused by heat

debris (duh-BREE) scattered pieces of something that has been wrecked or destroyed

embers (EM-burz) the hot, glowing remains of a fire

flammable (FLAM-uh-buhl) likely to catch fire

flee (FLEE) to run away from danger

goods (GUDZ) things that are sold

housing boom (HOU-zing BOOM) a time when many new houses are built

legend (LEJ-uhnd) a story passed down from earlier times that cannot be proved true

looting (LOOT-ing) stealing from stores or houses during a disaster

martial law (MAR-shuhl LAW) rule by an army during a time of disaster

morgue (MORG) a place where dead bodies are kept before being buried

prairie (PRAIR-ee) a large area of flat grassland

refugees (REF-yoo-jeez) people forced to leave their homes because of a disaster or war

soup kitchens (SOOP KICH-uhnz) places that give food to people in need

souvenirs (soo-vuh-NIHRZ) objects that remind people of something

temporary (TEM-puh-*rer*-ee) lasting for only a short time

timber (TIM-buhr) wood used for building

waded (WAYD-id) walked in or through shallow water

waterworks (WAW-tur-WURKS) a system of pumps and pipes that provides water to a community

weary (WIHR-ee) very tired

Bibliography

Bales, Richard F. *The Great Chicago Fire and the Myth of Mrs. O'Leary's Cow.* Jefferson, NC: McFarland & Company (2005).

Cromie, Robert. *The Great Chicago Fire.* Nashville, TN: Rutledge Hill Press (1994).

Kogan, Herman, and Robert Cromie. *The Great Fire: Chicago 1871.* New York: G. P. Putnam's Sons (1971).

Lowe, David Garrad, ed. *The Great Chicago Fire: In Eyewitness Accounts and 70 Contemporary Photographs and Illustrations.* New York: Dover Publications (1979).

Miller, Ross. *The Great Chicago Fire.* Urbana, IL: University of Illinois Press (2000).

Sawislak, Karen. *Smoldering City: Chicagoans and the Great Fire, 1871–1874.* Chicago: University of Chicago Press (1995).

Read More

Balcavage, Dynise. *The Great Chicago Fire.* Philadelphia: Chelsea House (2001).

Marx, Christy. *The Great Chicago Fire of 1871 (Tragic Fires Throughout History).* New York: Rosen (2004).

Murphy, Jim. *The Great Fire.* New York: Scholastic (1995).

Stein, R. Conrad. *The Great Chicago Fire (Cornerstones of Freedom, Second Series).* Danbury, CT: Children's Press (2005).

Learn More Online

To learn more about the Great Chicago Fire, visit **www.bearportpublishing.com/CodeRed**

Index

About the Author

Janet McHugh is a writer and editor who grew up in Chicago. Her grandfather was a captain in the Chicago Fire Department. Her granduncle was killed fighting a railroad fire on the site of what today is Chicago's famed Millennium Park.